COACH YOURSELF
BETTER, FAST

THE LISTENING
LEADER

Based on *The Listening Shift* by Janie van Hool

First published in Great Britain by Practical Inspiration Publishing, 2025

© Janie van Hool and Practical Inspiration Publishing, 2025

The moral rights of the author have been asserted.

ISBN   978-1-78860-759-9   (paperback)
         978-1-78860-760-5   (epub)
         978-1-78860-761-2   (Kindle)

Every effort has been made to trace copyright holders and to obtain their permission for the use of copyright material. The publisher apologizes for any errors or omissions and would be grateful if notified of any corrections that should be incorporated in future reprints or editions of this book.

EU GPSR representative: LOGOS EUROPE, 9 rue Nicolas Poussin, LA ROCHELLE 17000, France Contact@ logoseurope.eu

Want to bulk-buy copies of this book for your team and colleagues? We can customize the content and co-brand *The Listening Leader* to suit your business's needs.

Please email info@practicalinspiration.com for more details.

Contents

Series introduction

Welcome to *6-Minute Smarts*!

This is a series of very short books with one simple purpose: to introduce you to ideas that can make life and work better, and to give you time and space to think about how those ideas might apply to your life and work.

Each book introduces you to ten powerful ideas, but ideas on their own are useless – that's why each idea is followed by self-coaching questions to help you work out the 'so what?' for you in just six minutes of exploratory writing. What's exploratory writing? It's the kind of writing you do just for yourself, fast and free, without worrying what anyone else thinks. It's not just about getting ideas out of your head and onto paper where you can see them, it's about finding new connections and insights as you write. This is where the magic happens.

Find out more...

Introduction

As an only child, I became adept at participating in conversations with adults that were significant learning experiences. By listening to adult exchanges, I learned a few things to avoid and witnessed the drama being played out in the conversations around me. I spent a good deal of time alone, reading. Nothing helps us understand the perspective of others like a good book. Reading is listening – learning to understand the perspective of others while considering, reflecting and comparing world-views and exploring people's motivations.

This led me to a career as an actor that lasted for 12 years. I learned about the music of the voice and how to play it like an instrument to inform, to inspire, to create mood. I learned how to breathe, how to project confidence, how to manage stage fright. I learned to use my physicality as a way of creating characters and influencing audiences.

Having moved away from acting into voice studies and teaching, I had the opportunity to use my skills to shape and support a leadership team with their communication. I loved it and have now worked in this field for over 20 years. I have listened to diagnose, solve, shift and support. I have found ways to help leaders inspire with strategy, vision and storytelling.

Then, aged 50, I learned just to listen. I trained as a listening volunteer with the Samaritans – a UK charity dedicated to listening to people in distress and whose mission is to reduce the number of suicides by offering to simply listen... not to solve, give advice or offer a perspective, but rather to give another person the time and space to explore what's going on for them. Witnessing the transformational power of being heard has had the most profound impact on me.

Why listen as a leader?

The greatest value any leader can offer an organization is the ability to create the conditions that will enable people to be at their best. Businesses need emotionally intelligent leaders who have a competitive mindset with a compassionate heart.

Recent events have shifted where and how we work – a blend of office-based and remote working beckons and challenges us all. As technology advances, the importance of leaders who are able to connect to and understand their colleagues' perspectives, hopes and fears can't be overstated. In order for a business to be successful, its leaders must be able to ask the right questions and listen – deeply – to the answers.

Your people need a good listening to

If you listen well, you are setting another person up for success, and if you speak well, you are ensuring your listener will be able to listen well. Listening well reduces fear and resistance to change. It humanizes leadership, allowing people to connect through shared values and understanding. It fosters an environment of trust, increasing collaboration and creating a stronger commitment to teams.

Listening is an art, a skill, a practice, a commitment. It requires preparation, self-awareness and self-control. It demands curiosity, patience, generosity and a desire to understand.

Listening well brings customers to your door and keeps them on your side.

You're ready to start. Over the next ten chapters (ten days, if you fancy treating this as a mini-course), you're going to discover ten key principles of listening as a leader and experiment with using them for yourself.

Let's go!

Day 1
The 'why' of listening

We are all constantly involved in communication. Whether we are writing, reading, speaking or listening, we are engaging with others to learn, understand and progress our conversations. So, if it matters so much, we need to be exceptionally good at it, right?

Any expert will tell you that mastery involves practice, coaching and asking for help or feedback from a team of supportive, trusted advisors. It can't be achieved in a 45-minute webinar, a half-day workshop or a module on a development programme. Listening is important, but simply saying your intention is to listen doesn't mean you'll do it well. To do that, you need to put in the hard hours. To become an exceptional communicator, I urge you to start with learning to listen well, then think about how to help people listen to you.

Why is listening so hard?

Most of us are not taught how to listen – we are just told to do it. Few of us have had formal teaching in listening, so it's no wonder we find listening challenging. Barriers to listening well are not just psychological – you may be tired, cold, unwell or worried. Distractions come in all shapes and sizes – and they make listening hard.

Cultural influences on listening

Social media encourages us to put our lives online, curating and narrating a constructed version of how we live and insisting that others pay attention to us. In 2020, social media urged us to #BeKind following the tragic death of Caroline Flack; there were calls for people to listen to each other with compassion. But that recognition of the damaging impact of messages posted on social media doesn't seem to have changed anything on the listening front, sadly.

Voices may call for change and healthy dialogue may begin, but there still seems to be more talking than listening, more defensiveness than understanding – and consequently more harm still being done.

Part of this is down to our political system. All political parties are keen to be seen as listening, but the intention to listen is usually a cover for the opportunity to talk. 'Listening' is too often explaining, denying, changing the subject.

The challenges of political listening are similar to the issues faced when listening in businesses – the listening is likely to be selective. Our political leaders must pay attention to different voices and listen without defending. If the conversations we see played out in front of us, moderated by a journalist or interviewer, are simply an exchange of point and counterpoint, then we will all stop listening. Indeed, we may have done just that already!

Why does listening matter so much now?

There are immediate priorities calling for all of us to listen:

- The need for conversations about diversity: It's time to approach these conversations as partners, with concrete commitments to making change. Any hint of assumption, judgement or minimizing what's being said will damage relationships further. A business needs diversity of thought to be successful.

- The need for inclusion: As social creatures, people need to feel connected to others. Connection promotes well-being and enhances psychological safety. Listening with empathy, compassion and generosity makes people feel cared about – they feel that they matter. Concerns about communication are usually a red flag – a sign that people are feeling disconnected, uncertain, excluded. Listening to concerns without defensiveness or justification will start to build a bridge and signal a commitment to inclusivity as a priority.

- The need to enable people to talk about mental health: I have seen most of my client organizations make commitments to supporting mental health in the workplace. They encourage people to speak about their emotional experiences, aiming to make it completely fine to be honest about challenges, difficulties and struggles. But if we expect people to take this courageous step, we have to make sure that their *speaking up* is met with *being listened to* well. Anyone running a well-being programme in the workplace needs to have the right training and support to feel completely confident in their listening skills... and to know how to handle what they hear.

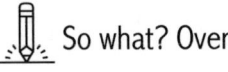 So what? Over to you...

1. What's the purpose of listening?

2. Who taught you to listen well? How?

3. How do you make yourself easy to listen to?

Day 2
The 'how' of listening

Listening needs to be continuous, always on... and, importantly, genuine.

Five ways to listen across your organization

1. Try a listening audit
    Think carefully about how your business works as a community. Here are some questions to ask so that you can understand how people feel:

    *   Do you feel listened to by the people who matter to you at work?
    *   What makes you feel heard?

- How could we listen better as an organization?

2. Find your listeners – and train them well
   Promote the initiative as a culture change programme, state its importance and then find out who's genuinely curious about listening to the views of colleagues. Look for people across every part of the business. Teach them using a specialist programme designed for your organization. This can use blended learning – online and face-to-face learning sessions supported by tools and peer support groups. Celebrate their contributions, holding them up as examples of excellence in your business culture and publicly acknowledging and appreciating what they do. If, as a leader, you are seen to value these skills highly, you'll create a positive ripple effect.

3. Start listening groups, run by your listeners
   Listening groups are similar to focus groups – a small sample of people sharing their thoughts about particular topics or aspects of the business. You aren't seeking to solve a problem, or even identify one. You are allowing people to share their experiences and have them acknowledged by others in

listening mode only – it's the sharing of stories. Our current methods of communicating in soundbites are starving us of this connected practice of storytelling.

4. Hold 'town halls' or 'all-hands' meetings

I have seen these events run as open Q&As, which can be successful, but this relies on a few big personalities speaking up on behalf of others. So, when organizing a meeting to listen to the people in your organization, try this approach instead:

- Ask for questions beforehand and respond to them. This will give you a good idea of the most pressing issues on people's minds.
- Put people into small groups for 10 to 15 minutes of conversation – approximately five or six people per group. Give them a theme related to your message and ask them to discuss and come up with one question per group, which can be either submitted in writing or asked in plenary by a nominated spokesperson.
- Offer a short presentation on the issues or ideas that come up, then separate people into small groups again to discuss further.

But this time have one of your team (better still, one of your listeners) facilitate so that they can listen more carefully. This needs to be a longer conversation – 30 minutes or so. Have a note-taker in each group submit findings – this may be done anonymously. Be crystal clear that you are having someone take notes because you want to understand the issues raised, and let people know the notes will not identify individuals. Contributors need to feel safe to speak up; otherwise you'll get polite commentary but nothing of real value.

- Create the conditions for people to interact creatively after the group discussion – this might be through public writing or recording areas where ideas can be shared in response to what has been heard. Genuinely commit to summarizing what you read/hear and responding in the coming days. Give people confidence that you will take their views on board.

5. Conduct a listening roadshow or tour

The senior leaders in your business – including the chair, the board and the non-executive directors – will benefit from regularly travelling to meet people across the business in person or connecting virtually to find out how people are feeling and to hear their ideas for positive and constructive change. The tone needs to be sincere and the process needs to feel meaningful. If you show patience with people, you will get to the heart of things.

Running a listening meeting

Meetings are a time-consuming and unavoidable feature of our working lives. They can work well and create understanding and productivity, fostering great team rapport. Conversely, there may be frustrations over how much time they take up and the preparation necessary for them.

Listening in groups is the biggest listening challenge of all owing to interpersonal dynamics, preferences in communication style and situational politics. It's easy to assume that others are listening, and it's easy for us to appear to be listening when our thoughts are elsewhere.

Creating the conditions for a listening meeting

Humans seem able to maintain focused attention for a matter of minutes before productivity declines, so try creating the optimum conditions for people to listen.

1. Find out how long people would like meetings to run for... and how much time they would appreciate between meetings to reflect and reset.
2. Find out what people want to discuss and what contributions they hope to make.
3. Make it possible to agree when, where and how the meeting could work best for them.
4. Aim for a meeting lasting only 15 minutes, then ask everyone to head off and consider the points or issues that have been raised.
5. Have people contribute to a shared document so as to continue the conversation between meetings.
6. Reconvene for another brief meeting at an agreed date to summarize the information gathered and agree next steps.

Clarity, brevity and collaboration are essential to the set-up, but the listening behaviour in a well-constructed meeting also matters. The speaker/ listener technique helps improve this.

The speaker/listener technique

Allow the listeners to focus carefully on what each speaker is saying, ensuring they demonstrate understanding. Each speaker should not talk for too long. Everyone should be respectful of others' right to say what they need to say.

Acknowledging to everyone present that this new technique will feel clunky at first will allow you all to continue to develop the method and strengthen your listening skill – along with enhancing meeting behaviour more generally.

Being heard is energizing. The important thing is to know how others are feeling, and if that yields the results you want, then you're on to a good thing. You could even try it with your friends and family!

Rules for the speakers

1. Speak for yourself, and don't mind-read.
   When we hear someone express a thought, it's tempting to guess what they mean rather

than asking them to clarify. So take care not to speak on behalf of others – listen instead.

2. Don't go on and on.

 Have you ever come across the acronym WAIT? It stands for 'Why Am I Talking?' This provides us with a useful check-in as we speak. (Or maybe you need to ask yourself WAIST? – 'Why Am I Still Talking?!') To be more aware of what works best, pay attention in your meetings to the length of time people take to express their views.

3. Stop often to allow the listeners to paraphrase. You may only need to do this when the subject is complex, potentially inflammatory or painful to engage with. But be mindful not to sound patronizing when you try this.

Rules for the listeners

1. Paraphrase what you hear – don't interpret. Paraphrasing is the method of playing back a short summary of the key points you've heard without interpreting them. Each speaker should pause to allow you to do this.

2. Don't interrupt or contradict – focus on what each speaker is saying.

In this process, you'll need to manage the desire to interrupt, correct or use phrases like 'Yes, but...'.

Rules for both

1. The speaker has the floor when they are speaking.
2. The listener has the floor when they are paraphrasing.
3. Ensure all voices are heard equally.

Allow each speaker to complete their thought process and say what they need to say, in short sections. Then allow listeners to paraphrase. You may find it helpful to nominate a facilitator to manage the conversation or use a physical object to indicate who has the floor.

Be patient – your turn will come...

How to keep getting better

Remember that when people's ideas, contributions and suggestions are not actioned, or where there is disagreement, they may easily feel that they have not been 'listened to'. So make sure others are properly heard and part of the conversation.

To help you succeed in developing listening meetings with the speaker/listener technique, set aside three minutes at the end of meetings to answer the following questions:

1. What went well using this technique?
2. What do we need to focus on to improve our next meeting?

Listening in virtual meetings

The speaker/listener technique also works well in online meetings, where individual contributions may be difficult to manage. People will appreciate being given the space to express themselves fully. Remote conversations make it difficult to read the full picture in terms of how others are feeling – what's known as a 'low-context' environment (more on this in Day 9). We can only make sense of the conversation based on what we see and hear. Using the speaker/listener technique will allow each person to say what they need to say and know that it has been heard and understood.

How the technique helps conversations about inclusion

Conversations about inclusion go straight to the heart of what can be so difficult about listening. It's uncomfortable to anticipate what we might hear and how we might feel when we hear it. The speaker/listener technique won't soothe those fears, but using it will ensure that the people in your business who have a right to be heard and who have something they need to say will feel, and be, heard.

 So what? Over to you...

1. How can I make my listening more genuine and consistent in my personal or professional life?

2. What simple actions could I take to foster a stronger culture of listening in my team or organization?

3. How might using the speaker/listener technique improve tough conversations or virtual meetings I'm part of?

Day 3
Mindfulness

Learning to listen to yourself

You're a busy person. I know that because of the research that tells us about organizational productivity, burn-out and the 'always on' culture we live in. Whether you're working remotely, in the office or a blend of the two, it's likely that you're under pressure, with a lot of unfinished tasks nagging away at you.

Being able to listen fully requires the discipline of parking distractions and being present for the conversation. It's hard to imagine anyone being able to listen effectively without learning how to become fully present.

Four ways to listen to yourself

1. Create space

Take therapy sessions, for example. These tend to be booked by the hour, but last only 50 minutes. Those precious ten minutes left to the therapist allow them the time to complete any notes, take a comfort break and, crucially, refocus themselves to prepare for their next session. This discipline serves both the therapist and the client, reducing 'rush' and allowing the practitioner to create an atmosphere conducive to listening.

2. Mind shift

When leaders address differences between leading and managing in training forums, it's fascinating to see them reflect on how addictive it is to get cracking on stuff they can tick off a to-do list. Think of these as puzzles, not problems.

Problems can be emotionally challenging – they can remain unresolved for a long time, take on a life of their own, continue to grow. *Puzzles* can give satisfying evidence of output, completion, achievement. Under pressure, it's human nature to revert to puzzles, where we can feel certain and avoid problems. This is the very opposite of what we need to be able to become present and listen well. But the pull of finishing stuff draws us away from a deeper conversation.

Have you ever tried to have a conversation with someone who's writing an email at the same time? It's transactional at best. There's no space to engage in the conversation from the listener's perspective, and the speaker's space is squeezed into micro-seconds of attention from the listener.

You can't engage fully unless you take the route of creating space for yourself to settle, feel prepared and consider the atmosphere you need to create.

How long do you need to centre yourself and be ready to listen? Only you can know. The first step is to check in with yourself.

- Am I solving puzzles or problems?
- What's my equivalent of the 50-minute hour and how can I make it work for me?

Creating space in the workplace can be hard – but it can be just as hard working from home with the multitude of distractions that are likely to draw your attention. Give yourself the best chance you can of listening to yourself by creating the space that works best for you.

3. Work out when and where you do your best thinking

Have a think about when and where you do your best thinking... It might be walking the dog, running, in the shower, in the car or in bed.

Perhaps these resonate with you? All the things I've listed are created by space – moments of regular, flowing movement or quiet, unpressured time when you can access deeper memories and when your brain waves are slower. These are the moments when we can really listen to ourselves and notice how we are feeling. In these moments, you are able to reflect on how you want to engage with others to solve some of the problems you face in your work.

4. Noticing

It will be difficult for you to notice what's going on for others as you listen to them if you find it hard to notice what's going on for you. This is the principle of self-awareness highlighted by Daniel Goleman in his book *Emotional Intelligence*.[1]

Goleman's model of emotional intelligence, also known as emotional quotient, has evolved over the years, but what seems to be a stable part of it is the ability to monitor our own emotions and those of other people.

As a listener, you benefit from noticing what emotions you are feeling so that you can choose how to deal with them. They may be emotions that arise as a result of how you feel about the person you are in conversation with or the effect a situation is having on you. It's vital to *notice*.

Mindfulness

Professor Mark Williams, former Director of the Oxford Mindfulness Centre, says that *mindfulness* means knowing what's going on inside and outside ourselves, moment by moment, as a way of increasing our ability to notice.

Another way to approach noticing is to consider our mindlessness. Reflecting on how automatically we respond in conversation, or how habitually we approach everyday situations, might help to redefine a methodology for noticing. Noticing is about not relying on 'automatic pilot' and not making assumptions. Keep your mind open by listening to yourself and others to keep curiosity, flexibility and agility at the heart of your decision-making.

Everyday practices to improve noticing

1. How am I feeling?

On a scale of 1 to 10, where 1 is low and 10 is the best you've ever felt, give yourself an instinctive number to reflect how you are feeling *right now*. Then unpick the reasons for being at that number – an exercise called 'Clearing Listening'.

- What's contributing to the overall score?
- Is it a physical assessment?
- Emotional?
- What's on your mind?

For example: '4 out of 10 today. I've been sitting down for too long, feeling stressed. Thinking about the conversation I had this morning and can't stop replaying it in my mind.'

This is a system of noticing what might get in the way of being fully present – listing all the things that are taking up space in your head and blocking your ability to notice anything else.

This exercise also works well with a word choice. Limit yourself to one word that sums up how you feel in the moment – be as instinctive as you can in choosing the word quickly. Then unpick why that word sprang to mind, using physical, emotional and mental insight.

2. Breathing

Paying attention to how you breathe will reap so many benefits. I have witnessed people in conversations holding their breath as they wait for the other person to finish talking – this is definitely not conducive to listening. And we are all aware of that wonderful sigh – the breathing out that we might experience as we arrive somewhere lovely to rest and recuperate. Breathing controls our emotional state, which influences our behaviour, and this is what influences those around us. It's worth managing this as a listener because how you breathe may be subconsciously influencing the conversation, and this can work both for you and against you.

Some breathing exercises are given below. For these, you may find it helpful to be on your own, sitting comfortably, eyes closed. But the exercises can be done anywhere as long as you can discipline yourself to focus in on the breath effectively.

- **Box breathing:** Breathe in for a count of four, hold your breath for a count of four, breathe out for a count of four, wait for a count of four. Repeat.

- **Four, seven, eight breathing:** Breathe in for a count of four, hold your breath for a count of seven, breathe out for a count of eight. Repeat four times.
- **Temperature breath:** A simple noticing exercise is to breathe in and out through your nose – easy, normal breathing, no extra effort required. As you breathe in, the air will feel cool as it enters your nostrils and warmer as you breathe out.

3. Noticing your surroundings – auditory

Sit or stand – as long as you're comfortable. Take a minute to adjust to the environment by being still and quiet. Then shift your attention to what you can hear in your immediate surroundings. Maybe nothing, maybe some familiar everyday sounds of technology working. Just notice. Then shift your attention a little further away – outside the room that you're in. Then further to outside the home or building you're in. Try to detect the furthest away sound you can possibly hear and all the sounds between, back to where you are at this precise moment.

This is a great way to become present – to become fully aware of your surroundings and be in the moment.

4. Noticing your surroundings – visual

- Look at the space you're in. Notice what you can about the environment and what's in it – how it's all laid out. Then look away or close your eyes momentarily. You're going to repeat this three times.
- Look at the space you're in again as if you are a child – maybe six or seven years old. What are the opportunities for fun and destruction in this space?
- Look at the space as if you are responsible for cleaning it – what's going to cause you effort and what's easy to break?
- Finally, look at the space as if you were a designer – what are the possibilities for changing it? What would cause you difficulties in your redesign and where's the potential for improvement?

You could take this exercise a stage further. If you have a big conversation with a colleague or customer, how might the environment either support or challenge the conversation's outcome?[2] How will the space look to the other person as they arrive?

I've heard many leaders say that their door is always open... but how will people feel when they walk in? Only noticing will give you the answer.

So what? Over to you...

1. How can I create more space in my day to listen to myself and be fully present?

2. What habits or routines help me notice my
   emotions, thoughts and surroundings more
   clearly?

3. When and where do I do my best thinking, and how can I make time for more of those moments?

Day 4
Empathy

Why empathy is helpful

Empathy tends to make us better listeners. Empathy is essential as a leader – understanding what life is like for people working across the business is key to building communities where people thrive and are able to – and want to – do their best work.

Social empathy

Social empathy requires us to understand what life is or has been like for a community where 'I know what you mean' is much less likely to have meaning. These are groups whose lives and experiences are not shared by us. We may have absolutely no idea what they have experienced, and this is where the harder work of listening kicks in as we try to understand without having any personal insight on the wider context.

This might mean listening to broaden our perspective about the lives of indigenous people, people of colour or the LGBTQ+ community, or listening to develop a better understanding of people who have experienced food poverty.

The challenge here is to probe the conversation not to understand how we might cope if we had been through similar experiences ourselves, but to reach a place of understanding where we realize what it has been like from the perspective of the other person. You need to really listen to put yourself into the shoes of the other person.

In your organization, benefit yourself and your employees by opening up conversations that encourage an honest appraisal of what life is like for the communities in your company. To be effective, these conversations will have to go beyond polite or managed messages. How will you demonstrate a commitment to listening – to hearing the truths that give you real perspective into your colleagues' lives?

Developing empathy

Flex your empathy muscle by drawing on your own experiences to find out how another person may be feeling – their experience may not be the same or directly connected, but you can use those emotions and senses you felt to connect to others.

A case study about Joe

Joe recently bought a small marketing business. Out of its 30 staff, he has to let 15 go. The remainder need to be integrated into Joe's existing team of 35 people, who are well-established, socially involved, long-time employees. Both sets of employees are naturally worried – for the existing employees, how will the culture of the business change, and for the new employees, how will life be working under new leadership, in a new office environment and with a new team?

How will Joe empathize with those involved and work towards supporting both sides?

Harnessing empathy

Joe recalls a childhood experience of leaving one town and moving to another, involving a change of school.

He left a close group of friends behind and knew no one in his new school. This affective memory, recalling how he felt, helps him connect with people in his business during this time of change. The two steps described below can help you recall past experiences.

Step 1: What emotions were felt?

Joe remembers feeling resentful towards his parents, extremely anxious and, initially, lonely.

Step 2: What sense memories are present?

- **Sight:** Joe recalls what he saw on his first day at the new school – buildings, faces, colours, shapes, sizes.
- **Sound:** He recalls what he heard – the radio station playing at home, the sounds of the family having breakfast before leaving for school, the playground noise before the bell rang to start school.
- **Smell:** He recalls the smell of coffee brewing and burnt toast at home, and he remembers the smell of bleach in the school corridors.
- **Taste:** He recalls his nerves, which made his breakfast toast taste like cardboard. He had a

metallic taste in his mouth from anxiety all morning, right up to lunchtime, when things started to improve and he enjoyed a cheese sandwich and an apple.

- **Touch:** He recalls giving his father a hug and not wanting to let go before leaving the house. He remembers being distracted and jamming his finger in his locker door and it stinging and then aching all day. He remembers sitting in his classroom on a hard chair. He remembers how smooth the keys on the keyboard in the computer room were as he typed.

Using your senses to connect to a memory allows for a powerful recall of an event that could otherwise be glossed over. For Joe, this is a route to empathy with his new team – remembering how new and unfamiliar things were and how isolating the experience of his first morning was.

Having done this exercise, Joe can listen to the concerns of those involved. Remembering his own emotional reaction in his situation takes away the fear of hearing others' emotions. He knows it's an unsettling time, but he can identify with people's feelings and will be able to demonstrate empathy as he listens.

Empathy questions

Joe might use the following questions to reflect on people's motivations and behaviours.

1. How do the other people perceive the situation?

    They might think this merger has been imposed on them and they're expected to work differently in the new team. Or they might think management is more focused on profit than employee happiness. Or that the new workload is going to create stress.

2. What might be troubling them?

    The staff from Joe's initial team might be wondering: Am I going to be replaced? What if the new team outperforms our existing one? Or they might be thinking that everything will change – it won't be the same place to work. Both groups might be thinking that as the business grows, more and more work is going to be pushed their way.

3. What emotions might they be feeling?

    Resentment, anxiety, hostility, overwhelm, apathy?

4. What might they need?
   Reassurance, clarity, regular communication, team-building, a steady pace? Don't try to do too much at once – be patient.

Taking it further: empathy mapping

Empathy mapping can help you deepen your understanding of other people's perceptions. Use the questions below to reflect on a key person in your life who you would like to build a better relationship with. What new perspective does this offer you?

1. What are people seeing?
2. What are they hearing?
3. What motivates them?
4. What scares them?
5. What do they think and feel?
6. What do they say?

What type of empathy seems right for the context?

- **Emotional empathy:** This is the propensity to feel what another person is feeling. It appears powerful, but it's not ideal for listening. We can easily be swept up in the emotion of the situation and then it becomes about us – we are seizing the experience and personalizing it.

- **Cognitive empathy**: This is a rational recognition of what someone is describing. It's feeling, but with a cool head.

For leadership listening, more objective analysis, using cognitive empathy, may allow you to listen in the moment and focus your attention on the other person rather than indulge in the emotions that move you.

Can you have too much empathy?

I notice that some of my clients who are highly empathetic worry far more than others about the impact they are making in their role. Concerns about how their messages will be received can be paralyzing.

Commercial decisions may also be harder if you are a highly empathetic person as you think deeply about the effect on others – for example, the effect that making people redundant will have.

However, it's important not to let this recognition that you can overdo empathy put you off developing it. Stay curious!

So what? Over to you…

1. How can I create space as a leader to truly understand what life is like for my team or organization?

2. What practical steps could I take to demonstrate empathy while addressing both individual and group concerns?

3. How might I use empathy to guide decision-making without letting it hinder my ability to lead effectively?

Day 5
Listening

If we feel we already know how a person will respond, then what's the point of asking the question? All too often, it seems that we don't ask, or if we ask at all, we don't listen to the response because we've already processed what we assume it will be.

Let's think about the simple question 'How are you?' – this may often be answered with a standard 'Fine, thanks', because you can tell that the person asking the question isn't really available to listen to the answer. It's a habit, a social convention, a way of getting into the meat of a conversation that would be weird without this fleeting, cursory 'hello'. But if we start a conversation by paying so little attention, it's going to be difficult to turn up the dial as we continue the discussion. Start as you mean to go on.

Try using this checklist as a way of noticing your usual approach of asking 'How are you?' and taking it to the next level as a listener.

1. Check in with yourself... are you ready to pay attention? To notice? To listen?
2. Decide to be present.
3. Ask the question.
4. Notice what they say in response and how they say it – pay close attention to the full context of words, tone of voice, body language, facial expression, energy.
5. If you get a standard reply – 'Fine, thanks' – probe a little deeper... see whether you can uncover what 'fine' really means to them. Try asking something like 'What's fine on a scale of 1 to 10?'
6. Offer an observation – 'I noticed a spring in your step this morning!' or 'You're walking a little slower than usual today... deep in thought?'

These small observations are an indication of your desire to notice the other person. Using follow-up questions allows people to become fully engaged and feel valued.

Next, let's think about some scenarios.

Listening to support

Colleague: I've got so much on at work right now. Not sure how I'm going to cope.

Manager: That sounds tough. What's the biggest challenge?

Create the space for the other person to investigate and express how they are feeling. You're focusing the conversation on them – not on yourself.

Listening to switch back to ourselves

Colleague: I've got so much on at work right now. Not sure how I'm going to cope.

Manager: Ugh – I know. You should see what's just landed on my desk this morning. Would it help to talk things through?

This might lead to a conversation that helps both manager and colleague. As long as balance is observed and they listen well to each other, this may be exactly what they both need to manage their respective situations.

Listening to solve

> *Colleague*: I've got so much on at work right now. Not sure how I'm going to cope.

> *Manager*: Right. Well first of all you need to get on top of the main account, then you should meet with the team on Slack this afternoon and let them know what you're not going to be able to deal with before it all gets out of hand.

In this case, the manager's response of solving the problem removes all autonomy from the colleague. This may increase their stress as they might feel that the manager thinks they're not capable of doing the job.

Not being listened to well, or not feeling that you've been heard, can be stressful. It triggers frustration and feelings of being undermined and rejected. If two people in conversation are competing to listen, it's not going to be much of a conversation! Most of the time, whatever our contribution, we are seeking to be heard and acknowledged.

It might help you to categorize your relationships as follows:

- Casual interactions: These might be occasional conversations with people you have very little need to develop a personal or professional relationship with.

- Relationships with **your team or work colleagues**: These are frequent conversations with people you collaborate with, influence and engage, but you may not know much about their personal lives, focusing on daily transactions and tasks to get the job done rather than more intimate or personal conversations.

- Social relationships: These are friends, neighbours – people you have longer and deeper connections with. You may or may not see them often, but they are valued by you and people whose company you would choose.

- Relationships with **your inner circle**: These are your most immediate relationships with a partner and close family and friends. They are the people you interact with most frequently, and your most important relationships are with them.

Try asking a couple of trusted colleagues, friends or family members what they experience in you as a listener. Such honesty may feel uncomfortable, but their responses may lead to a great conversation. All you have to do is listen!

What's your approach to listening?

Rate yourself using both words and numbers. Don't overthink it – your instinctive assessment will ensure you avoid any justification that may prevent you from taking action.

Ten steps to listening well

Step 1: Manage the judge

It's an evolutionary instinct to judge other people – but let go of that judgement.

In my work with the Samaritans, it'd be hard to find empathy if I've already decided that the caller is in some way unworthy of my understanding because I disapprove of their choices in life. It's not for me to judge, no matter what I hear.

In organizations, where time and opportunity to talk may be limited because of the sheer number of tasks that need to be completed, judging may seem a shortcut to getting things done.

If you're going to commit to improving your listening, notice how you're feeling and what's going on for you, then take responsibility for it.

Step 2: Be curious, not certain

This step is non-negotiable. It's a must-do, a muscle to flex, a committed, minute-by-minute promise to become an inquirer. Developing a mindset of curiosity will help you listen and be interested by what you hear. More and more questions will pop into your mind and the conversation will flow.

If we can ask questions to build a more detailed picture, to develop our understanding of the complexity of the situation, to investigate the range of emotions a person may be experiencing, not only will we have listened well, but they will feel heard and understood.

Step 3: Ask interested questions

Try reframing the familiar phrase 'open questions' as 'interested questions' as it emphasizes the importance of curiosity in conversation.

The inference of an open question such as 'Why didn't you use the model I showed you?' is obvious and will lead to someone becoming temporarily defensive and awkward. You could rephrase it to an interested question like 'Will you tell me about the model you used?'

As a leader, try to have key questions prepared and think carefully about how to make them work for the listener before falling into the trap of getting the tone wrong. We need the time to think about what to ask and how to express it rather than diving in without considering the pitfalls first.

It's important to recognize that skilful questioning is not simply a matter of starting a sentence with who, what, when, where, why or how. A direct, closed question can trigger a powerful response that may start the conversation with energy. You might ask, 'Are you clear about what you want to get from this conversation?' The answer must be a version of 'Yes', 'I think so', 'Not really' or 'No'. Whatever the answer, it's helpful because the next question can be an expression of interest – you'll want to find out what's behind the response.

Going a little deeper

We enjoy being asked interested questions – after all, it shows the other person's curiosity and gives us a chance to share our views, tell our experiences, give our opinions. You may want to use the TED acronym to allow the conversation to deepen and become richer.

T – 'Tell me...'
E – 'Explain...'
D – 'Describe...'

The pressure to ask lots of questions in a conversation with a person or group you've never met before can be inhibiting, but the TED approach will encourage other people to speak at length. Then you'll have great material to help you ask follow-up questions.

Step 4: Interrupt mindfully

Psychology professor Han Li from the University of Northern British Columbia uses the following definitions in her research on cultural differences in interrupting.[3] Take a look at them and consider how you might interrupt others.

Cooperative interruptions

- **Agreement:** showing enthusiasm and support for the speaker's ideas

- **Assistance:** if the speaker forgets a word or what they were about to say
- **Clarification:** to check understanding

Intrusive interruptions

- **Disagreement**: jumping in to voice a different view
- **Floor-taking:** taking over the conversation but staying on the same subject
- **Topic-changing:** cutting in to change the subject
- **Summarization:** paraphrasing the speaker's point and often minimizing it

Cooperative interruptions fit nicely with the concept of listening to support, whereas intrusive ones switch the conversation away from the speaker to satisfy another's agenda. Notice how your colleagues interrupt. Is it to encourage or expose? What's the point of building an argument for an idea and preparing to present it with passion and enthusiasm if you then have it rigorously unpicked before getting the chance to paint the full picture?

Step 5: Acknowledge, encourage and appreciate

In all areas of my life, both professional and personal, I've noticed that conversations work best where there is acknowledgement and appreciation from both sides – when you're letting each other know you've been seen and heard.

As a coach, I'm deliberate about encouraging and appreciating my clients for stepping outside what feels comfortable for them and exploring what's possible. If I do that well, I know that the next time I encourage them, they'll take even bigger leaps forward.

At the Samaritans, we are encouraged to appreciate our callers for taking the step to contact us and to share important personal experiences. We encourage our callers to keep talking if it helps – it's a way of showing that we want to listen, we are present and we care.

As a leader, acknowledging the contributions of others can easily be achieved by making short public statements like 'I think that's right', 'You make a good point', 'Thanks for highlighting that for us'.

Step 6: Value the sound of silence

Silence is golden, as the expression goes, and that may be true of some blissful quiet moments on your own somewhere lovely, but it's not a fitting description of the heavy canopy that descends when two people sit opposite each other in silence during a painful or challenging conversation.

We may be silent because we are afraid of what we are about to hear and how we might feel when we hear it. Once you get used to silence, though, you begin to realize the immense value of it as a listener. You begin to relax – you don't have to drive the conversation, but instead can wait for an offer from the other person. Just wait... they will say something, and it'll probably be something you didn't expect.

Solitary silent reflection can be transformative, but it can also lead to rumination. Having another person there as we think requires us to draw the themes together and find a way of expressing our thoughts out loud. Then we get a reaction, understanding and an opportunity to take our thinking to the next step.

Practising silence

Here are a few ways you can practise silence.

1. Notice how generous others are in giving you the space and silence to reflect in conversation with them. How do you feel if someone interrupts your flow of thought to give advice, ask diverting questions or bring the conversation back to themselves?

2. Confess to someone you trust that you're having a go at improving your use of silence.

    *   Set up a five-minute conversation where you ask someone about their week or something light so that you can concentrate on the task rather than worry about the content. Let them speak until they naturally finish – no interrupting.
    *   Before responding, count to five. Ask whichever probing questions you are curious to hear the answer to. Let them talk again.
    *   Repeat using the count to five until the conversation reaches a conclusion.

3. Ask a trusted work colleague to join you for a walk. Invite them to talk about something that's on their mind and tell them you'll

be listening to them and not interrupting, questioning or commenting. Tell them they have eight minutes to share their situation and thoughts about it. They will take a couple of minutes to share what's on their mind and then will run out of content. And that's where silence comes in...

- Wait, walking side by side in silence.
- Without prompting, after 30 seconds or so they will start talking again, and during this round of speaking, they'll uncover insights or share more deeply than in the first round, when they were just setting the context.
- Keep going until you reach the full eight minutes.
- Then spend two minutes reflecting on what you heard.

4. Start to notice what happens to your conversations more generally as you deliberately use silence. Silence is a key factor in creating presence and developing gravitas – you won't get to be a great listener without finding silence. It will also give you the space to think about the next few steps.

Step 7: React

Reacting to what you hear is critical to the other person's experience of being heard. None of us wants to feel that we've been courageous enough to voice a view or share what matters to us only for it to be ignored or dismissed. As a manager, you need to react if you are going to demonstrate good listening. The following phrases are useful for showing a reaction, but not assuming:

- 'That sounds...' – for example, 'That sounds like a terrible morning.'
- 'That seems...' – for example, 'That seems to have built to quite a list of things to deal with.'

But the most important thing is to be in the moment, respond like a human being and show compassion and understanding – show that you've noticed and that you care.

Step 8: Repeat what you hear

Reflecting is a method of repeating back words or phrases that you hear the speaker using. While initially it may feel a bit mechanical and clunky, it's actually transformative. Sometimes you can play back something that has just been said by the speaker and they'll exclaim, 'Yes! That's right!' almost as if they had no idea that the words had come straight out of their own mouth. That's a magic moment – your conversation has become a listening exchange.

Step 9: Check your understanding

Check that you've understood what's said accurately.

1. When *listening*, we can too easily fall into the trap of assuming we understand what's being said. This is evident when we use intrusive interruptions or try to switch the conversation back to our own agenda.

   Try these signposting phrases to check your understanding:
   - 'Let me check that I've got this right...'
   - 'Can I clarify a couple of points...?'
   - 'For my benefit, could we revisit...?'

2. When speaking, we often behave as though we have the listener's full attention, though we know that this is variable at best.

   Ask your listeners to play back to you any points, reactions or thoughts that would help you know that everyone is clear on what you've said. Soften the challenge by suggesting you might have over-complicated, talked too much or covered too many points, and request hearing things from their perspective as a means of ensuring that you're communicating clearly. Avoid the direct 'Are we all clear, then?' unless you can be sure that there is enough trust in the room to express doubt or uncertainty. If people have only half listened, and half 'got it', mistakes are likely to be made.

Step 10: Summarize

As a Samaritan, I've noticed that a person's story can take a while to tell – it will have many elements and characters and will often cover a long period of time, so summarizing little and often is helpful.

In your meetings and conversations, it can be helpful to think in episodes and chapters. The practice of catching up as we go along does four things well:

1. It helps the speaker feel sure that they are being heard.
2. It takes the pressure off the listener to grasp everything that's being said.

3. It reduces the need for note-taking, which keeps the connection and focus alive between speaker and listener.
4. It allows the listener to pick up on particular sections of the story to develop depth of understanding.

Summarizing also allows you, as a listener, to express what you've heard in your own words. This is a sure sign that you've not only listened, but also understood.

So what? Over to you...

1. How could I approach a tricky conversation this week with more curiosity and presence and fewer assumptions?

2. What steps can I take to create space for silence and reflection in conversations, especially during challenging discussions?

3. How can I better show others that I've understood and valued their perspective through summarizing or thoughtful reactions?

Day 6
Being relevant

Imagine a scenario: A well-known UK brand was bought out by a US investor and huge changes were rapidly imposed on the business, with many people being made redundant. The leadership communicated the rationale for the changes, but it wasn't enough and those that were still employed felt unsure about their roles. The financial aspiration of the business and a rationale for action was the only aspect the leadership had considered.

What do you think would have been relevant for the colleagues in the business? What was on their minds? How would you feel walking out on a 15-year career knowing that although you had lost your job, shareholder value would ensure a bonus in the years to follow for those lucky enough to have an investment in the company?

The assumption made here is that people would want to know, where possible, what was happening and why.

But, actually, there was a need for people to know how their lives were going to be affected, whether they stayed in the business or left it.

So overlooking what people need to know caused great difficulties – a culture of frustration, anxiety, apathy and denial grew by the day. The leadership assumed they knew what would be relevant to their people and imposed it on them. They failed to consider what mattered to their listeners, and this made what they did share too hard to listen to.

You have to be sure that people will see the information you share as *relevant to them*.

Rules for relevance

Our starting point for any communication with anyone has to be finding out what's relevant for them. This is empathy in action.

- What do you think is relevant to your people?
- How have you built this view of what's relevant?

- What views, decisions and ideas are you imposing on people?
- Whose voices do you never get to hear first hand?
- How can you find out what matters to them?

Think of three people who are important to you. Try to identify people who are different – on the basis of gender, age, cultural background and so on.

Then consider this statement: 'Climate change is relevant to all of us because we all live on the planet.'

This type of statement is intended to galvanize people into action – but that's an assertion, and people may not respond the way we'd like them to. The statement itself may be true, but that doesn't necessarily make it relevant to individual listeners. It needs tailoring to allow it to resonate with different people for different reasons.

1. How would you recreate this statement to make it relevant to your three important people?
2. What angles would you take?
3. What examples would you give?
4. What language would you use?
5. What style of delivery would you choose?

Three tools for relevance

Your priority in making your messaging relevant for your listeners is to ask them what they want and need. This might be before you make a speech at a conference or a presentation to your customers or colleagues, or before you plan an agenda for a meeting. Ask... and listen.

If you don't commit to this approach, you risk becoming predictable in content and style. Predictable presentations and meetings are dull experiences that are way too much work for listeners.

1. Give your listeners a reason to listen.
2. Identify metaphors that will connect to their experience.
3. Tell their stories to show that you have listened to them.

Giving your listeners a reason to listen

There are so many ways to do this, ranging from dramatic to conversational. Always ask yourself 'Why should they listen?'

1. Answer the question you know they want answered (ask them what that is first).

2. Make a shock statement.
3. Use humour.
4. Ask questions – rhetorical or otherwise.
5. Tell a story.
6. Offer numbers that are relevant to them.
7. Use media – video, music, images.
8. Share quotes.
9. Be silent – long enough to build anticipation.
10. Change the environment in which you communicate – be bold, creative and surprising.
11. Show a news headline.
12. Use props.

Using metaphors to connect to other people's experience

Metaphors allow us to develop a shared language that helps us understand a situation. To explore what experiences people in your business are having, ask them to use a metaphor – this could yield surprising and fascinating insights.

Commonly used metaphors in organizations

Some metaphors pop up time and again in business communication, resulting in diminished relevance. For example:

- **Referring to 'going on a journey':** The communicator will tend to rely on the single word 'journey' to do the work, without extending the metaphor to build a compelling vision.
- **Referring to 'climbing a mountain':** This is a difficult metaphor to use if you want to create positive engagement – not many of us have climbed a mountain, and those who have will doubtless tell us how terrifying it is!
- **Referring to 'going into battle':** This can be a risky metaphor to 'deploy' if your aim is to engage and unify – after all, war is dangerous and casualties are many.
- **Talking about sport:** Sport metaphors can work, but they can also exclude a large part of your audience because sport is just not relevant to them.
- **Using mixed metaphors:** Combining metaphors is confusing and can both lose the listener and weaken the message.

Recently, the metaphors I've seen used in print and social media seem to be changing. I detect a movement from a strategy of push to a tactic of pull – engaging the heart, using a compassionate mindset, demonstrating empathy for people.

Unifying metaphors, like building bridges, drawing maps, shaping futures. Positive and optimistic visions of a sustainable world – homes, not houses; communities, not cities; nurturing and supporting, not driving and chasing. Metaphors that show ethical, moral, values-driven leadership.

Telling your listeners' stories

Your organization will doubtless have wonderful examples of strategy in action, a supportive culture, overcoming adversity, challenging the status quo and so many others. They are out there – you just need to find them and make them relevant to your audience. For example:

- Do you have year-end statistics to share? Tell a story about what these numbers mean for some of your colleagues and customers personally. What's changing – for good or bad? What will satisfy the burning questions they need answered?

- Is there a new strategy? This will affect the lives of everyone in the business, so tell stories about the evolution of the strategy – how it started, how it developed, who in your business you want to thank for the inspiration and for making it happen.
- Do you have product success to share? Tell your audience about the working lives of people in the plants and factories who make your product. Bring that community into the room and connect everyone to them.

Not all relevant stories have to be ground-breaking! There's also relevance in everyday, personal micro-experiences and fleeting moments, and sharing these will show just how committed you are to being connected to your community.

How to tell someone else's story

1. When you hear a story that you know is relevant to your people, find the highs and lows in the story flow and work around them. Reflect on the life of a person you know well and list three high points and three low points you know they've experienced. Think

about how you'd build a narrative around those events.

2. Bring the characters to life – if you name them (real or otherwise) and tell us that they're a grandparent, sister or son with values we may share and struggles we understand, you will be offering the details that make relevance happen. We feel affinity and connection with people whose lives mirror our own in some way. Consider including the following:

   - their name
   - their stage of life
   - their family circumstances
   - how they sound when they speak
   - how they look
   - their attitude to life
   - how they relate to your business

3. Include tiny details – pick one or two moments in your story that bring the narrative to life with the kind of details that make the experience real.

   - Describe a room or location in close detail so that we can visualize it.
   - Describe what someone's wearing in detail.
   - Describe an object in detail.

Keep the conversation going – ask for input and feedback, and reflect and review as often as you can to be sure that you're keeping the content of your conversations and presentations relevant for your listeners.

 So what? Over to you…

1. How can I better understand what is truly relevant to my team's needs and concerns before sharing important information?

2. What stories or metaphors could I use to make a message more meaningful and relatable for different individuals or groups this week?

3. Who in my organization or circle might have perspectives I've overlooked, and how could I engage with them to uncover what really matters to them?

Day 7
Showing and sharing the struggle

The value of sharing stories

Embracing the concept of struggle positively will help others listen for two reasons:

1. Stepping away from scripts, slides, board papers or rigid agendas can inject energy and presence into communication as you struggle, or strive, to find the right language and tone to engage your listeners.
2. No one sails through life without a struggle. While this may have created difficulty at times in your life, when others hear about it, it makes you very easy to listen to.

By listening to other people's struggles you open a window on your own values and motivations, making your purpose meaningful so that others will share it.

Talking about struggle is full of intensity. It's communication just at the edge of discomfort. It's exciting. It's unpredictable. It's real. That's always compelling to listen to.

Some of us are happier than others to open the doors to our private world, but it's important to do this in a way that feels right for you. As you reflect on the options below, be sure that you're comfortable with the examples you decide to use and that you'll feel at ease emotionally when sharing them.

A note of caution – this will work brilliantly, but *only* if you're committed to careful planning and preparation and rely on the good techniques we'll explore next.

Telling your own story

Build your book of relevant stories to share

It's important to be prepared. Use a notebook and write your thoughts in longhand – that will help them to stick. Jot down anything that comes to mind that could be useful. The following list may help you file your ideas, providing categories so you can choose a relevant experience to share when you need to. The categories are inspired by Annette Simmons, in her book *The Story Factor*.[4]

- **Who you are:** Your listeners will want to know who's in the room with them – tell stories about you, your influences, your background and what has inspired you.
- **What you've done:** Your listeners will want evidence that they can trust you – what can you tell them to demonstrate that their working lives are in safe hands? How have you come to this point and what have you done to prove yourself?
- **What motivates you:** Your listeners will want to understand your values, especially the leadership ethos that will guide them.
- **What your purpose is:** Your listeners will be curious about how you will lead them into the future, following a purpose, a vision, a mission.
- **How you care for people:** Your listeners will need to hear about experiences you've had in your life that demonstrate how well you understand theirs.
- **How you bounce back:** Your listeners will want to be inspired by knowing how you

overcome adversity, which inevitably raises its head from time to time – what did you learn?

Useful plots around which to build your stories

In his book, *The Seven Basic Plots: Why We Tell Stories*, Christopher Booker presents an analysis of stories and their themes.[5] I have chosen four that you might find helpful in telling stories of struggle to inspire your listeners:

1. Going from **rags to riches:** Think about the story of Cinderella. Have you ever started from scratch and made a success of something – transforming your life? Telling this story helps listeners feel inspired.

2. **Overcoming the monster**: Think about James Bond. Have you ever felt fear? Experienced self-doubt? Lost sleep worrying about a situation? Sharing what happened to bring you to where you are now will help your listeners feel they're in safe hands with a leader who has learned from experience.

3. Completing a **quest:** Think about the film *The Hobbit*. Starting a story with a vision for how it ends is a classic approach to engaging

listeners with purpose. You will all jointly navigate the ups and downs, and support each other through them. It's also a way of keeping the story evolving over time and letting it be co-created by all involved.

4. Experiencing **rebirth:** Think about the film *Groundhog Day*. This is a perfect example of a rebirth story. Have you ever repeated a mistake? Have you repeatedly taken the same approach to solving a problem until one day you realized you simply had to find another way? The plot of this film inspires change and the desire to lead your listeners through it.

How to tell your story

Sharing your struggle will build your credibility among your listeners. It will help them realize that you understand them and relate to their experience and that you care enough about them as people to open yourself up and introduce who you really are. You hold the keys to the door, which you can open as much or as little as you like.

Here are two ways to keep your listeners on the edge of their seat:

Showing and sharing the struggle

1. **Give them the last line first:** Decide what the last line of your story is and start with it. Then tell the story and finish with the line again. Don't explain the line or carry on past it. Think of it as the wrapping around a box.

2. **Use the senses:** Create a scenario five years from now by imagining that you are walking into your business with a prospective or new client. What do you see, hear, smell, feel? Try this exercise on your own or through facilitation with a team or group. You might want to let your mind wander or write down your thoughts and revisit them over a period of time. Try not to rush... let the sensory experience unfold until you feel you've really 'got it'. The richer the sensory picture, the more you'll enable people to listen, engage and envision their future in your business.

Whichever approach you choose, you must include the point of the story, or its moral. The moral will teach your listeners something that will spark change. Hearing the journey will inspire them to think, feel or behave differently. Avoid rambling as your message will be lost. Ensure you have a clear end point so you know where you're going and why you're heading there.

It can be helpful to announce that you're setting up the key point of the story – you might say 'The moral is...' or 'Why am I telling you this?'

Let's think about TED talks. Story-driven to engage and inspire learners, the TED approach expects communicators to do better than just read data from a slide. They need to become storytellers.

TED talks make the content relevant for listeners. They are full of struggle, and they are structured, crafted and rehearsed. TED speakers know how to make their content easy to listen to, and they always have a point of transformation at the end – the moral of the story.

Making sure you have that in place as you speak will ensure that your listeners are hanging on to the end of the story as it unfolds and that they get it. They get the point... and they'll take action because of it.

So what? Over to you...

1. What personal story of struggle or growth could I share with my team to help them better connect with my leadership purpose and values?

2. How can I prepare and structure one piece of communication this week to ensure it has a clear moral or transformation that inspires action?

3. How could I incorporate sensory details or relatable experiences into my communication to make it more engaging and memorable?

Day 8

Structuring the listening

The more structuring you do as you plan to communicate, the more likely it is that your listeners will hear what you've said and understand it. It's about clarity, brevity and simplicity.

1. You'll know exactly what it is you want to say and can be sure you'll say it.
2. You'll use fewer words and more pauses between content to allow the listener to absorb the message.
3. You'll appear certain. This inspires confidence in the listener, making them want to hear more.

4. You'll know how you're going to end the presentation or conversation. This gives your content a sense of direction and purpose.

Let's think about structure to help your listeners listen in two key areas: presentations and conversations.

Structuring a presentation

Slide presentations have become ubiquitous in business. But does a presentation help people listen? It depends... and a good deal of what it depends on is how you structure the presentation and slide content.

Does this look familiar?

I'm going to make a guess here that many of you will have built a presentation for your listeners in the following way:

1. You decided what you needed to say.
2. You started to build a deck of slides from a template.
3. You added content – to ensure you didn't forget anything.
4. You asked for input from a colleague or senior stakeholder.

5. You incorporated their additional content.
6. You added some images.
7. You added any notes at the bottom – source references, explanations, etc.
8. You put in a slide at the end saying 'Any Questions?'
9. You did a walk-through on the stage, probably the day before.
10. On the day, you ended up reading from the slide to be on the safe side, overrunning by ten minutes.

But where's *the listener* in all this?

You lost them when they realized you were reading out loud; when they sensed you would be overrunning, encroaching on their coffee break; when they couldn't follow what you were saying because it was so hard to know where you were heading.

A starting point for structure

To make a message easy to listen to, we need to know *exactly* what it is we are trying to say – *exactly* what it is we want people to hear and remember.

Before you plan any presentation, challenge yourself to decide how you would deliver the whole thing in seven words. The rules are:

- It makes sense when you say it – it's not seven random words.
- Anyone could understand it – no business jargon, just plain English!

Before you try this with a business message, have a go at the following exercises to help you realize that every story – and every message – has an essence you can build from.

Easy practice

Think of a favourite film – anything that springs to mind will be suitable. Try to summarize the story of this film in seven words. There are some rules:

- Focus on the story of the film.
- Don't include the title, catchphrases, actor names or character names.
- Don't use the phrase 'A film about...'

Here are three examples to start you off:

1. Wrongly convicted banker escapes jail through sewers (*The Shawshank Redemption*)
2. Shark kills beachgoers, is hunted and shot (*Jaws*)

3. Wicked stepmother loses stepdaughter to dancing prince (*Cinderella*)

Harder practice

Start by watching what is one of the most viewed TED talks: Daniel Pink's 'The puzzle of motivation'.[6] See how you might summarize it in seven words.

Apply the same rules.

- Focus on the overarching story Pink shares.
- Don't use the title of the presentation.
- Don't use the phrase 'A presentation about...'

Next, see whether you can summarize the story of one of your own presentations in seven words – for example, 'Enhancing our customer-centric mindset by focusing on core competencies' could be 'Offering brilliant service with a simplified range'.

Once you're sure you have your core message, you can build it out using structure.

A structure to lean on

I'm going to use Aristotle's three principles of persuasion, which ensure people are able to listen:

Structuring the listening

1. **Logos:** This appeals to the listener's logic or reason. Structure your argument and provide supporting evidence.
2. **Ethos:** This demonstrates your personality. Show the listener who you really are, conveying your expertise and why they should listen to you as someone with credibility in the subject.
3. **Pathos:** This appeals to listeners' emotion. Your ability to affect how your listeners feel is key here. If you demonstrate emotion, they will be more likely to feel the same.

The structure

Reason to listen

Set expectations

Theme 1	Theme 2	Theme 3

Conclusion

Reason to listen

Establish relevance, and be creative, brave, open and challenging – anything that provokes an emotional reaction will do the job as long as you can make it relevant.

Set expectations

Tell the audience what's coming. Use *a few* sentences to tell them what the purpose is, how they will feel as they hear it and how long you'll take. Then dive in.

Three main themes

The key skill in preparing a presentation is not about what content we put into it, but what we leave out. Choose three areas as the priorities.

Top tip! If you decide what you want to say and then walk away from your planning, try to recall everything you'd decided on. This will be the stuff you need to include. If *you* can't recall details from your plan, your listeners are unlikely to either. Remember to stay on theme.

Conclusion

Don't end with 'Any other questions?' There's nothing in that statement that tells me how I should leave the room feeling or what I should do as a result of listening to you.

Think about whether you want action or reaction? Maybe both... but use the opportunity to decide on this at the start of your planning process. Then you'll know where you're heading as you speak. And your listeners will leave having heard – and remembered – the most important part of the message.

Structuring a conversation

The exchange in a conversation matters – we need a balance between expressing what we want to say and enabling the other person to have the same experience.

Conversations that might be a difficult moment for a leader may be some of the standout moments of the listener's life – a conversation they never forget. So let's make sure those conversations are remembered for the right reasons.

Must-dos

1. Get the essential message across to the listener.
2. You need to know they've understood the message by taking responsibility for the way you articulate the message.

Start by asking yourself these three questions before you decide how to structure the conversation:

1. What do I want to happen?
2. What do I not want to happen?
3. How do I want them to feel?

How to give a perspective so that the listener hears it

You can take two routes to structuring a message, depending on its nature and who it's for.

1. Leave the receiver in no doubt about the request but also feeling valued.
   - Get straight to the point.
   - Offer an appreciative route forward.
2. Plan how to set the scene for the conversation using the following model:

I like...	A positive appreciation of the other person's efforts, qualities, intentions, etc. can go a long way towards making the conversation relaxed.
I don't like...	You now have the legitimacy to raise an issue – but only one. Keep it clear and brief.
I feel...	Own it. Identify the impact on you. Don't use 'I feel that you...', but rather 'I feel...'
I want...	Go for it. In one sentence, tell them exactly what you want going forward.
If you do...	These are the positive consequences – the potential outcome if the new behaviour or change is adopted. Include what's in it for them as well.
If you don't...	These are the negative consequences – the likely outcome of not taking action. Include what they can expect if they are unwilling to move forward.

How to say no so the listener hears it

If you have no problem saying no, I encourage you to think about how you express it – this can be an example of when a message can be too straightforward, causing hurt and offence when none may be intended.

Instead of just coming out with it, try the following structure:

Acknowledge the feelings of the other person.	It's important to prime them for the impact. Make this your own, but test out a statement like 'I know this is difficult to hear...'
Give them the message.	'I'm going to say no.' 'It has to be no.' 'Unfortunately, it's a no.'
Explain why the answer's no.	Limits need to be applied here. One reason *only* is sufficient – more than that and we lose the impact of the message or confuse the listener.
Offer a route forward.	This could be an alternative suggestion or an offer of support or resources – see whether you can think of something that eases the other person away from the disappointment of hearing 'no'.

A general rule about structure

The point of structure is to use it to enable fluency. It frees you to be present, 'in the moment', rather than worrying about what's coming next in your presentation or what you should say or ask to move the conversation forward.

A shift in responsibility

Responsibility lies with the speaker... it's our job to make the information clear, memorable, inspiring. If they missed the point, that's on us.

Ask yourself, 'What could I have done differently?' Ask them what they would like done differently and how you can help them listen well in the future. Painful though the feedback may be, it's what will allow you to make a difference and grow as a communicator.

So what? Over to you...

1. Think about a specific presentation, meeting or conversation in the week ahead. How can you simplify and structure your key messages to ensure clarity, brevity and impact for your audience?

2. What might you do to ensure your audience feels valued while still delivering the essential message or request clearly?

3. How could you use a seven-word description to make your next communication more memorable and actionable?

Day 9
Vocals and choreography

Your voice matters

Research by Professor Albert Mehrabian found that when there is inconsistency between the words spoken and the tone of voice or physical gestures, participants rely far more on the non-verbal communication than the actual words. The study was based on a woman saying nine single words but changing her body language and voice with each delivery.[7]

- Men *and* women will raise the pitch of their voices in social situations (or when talking to babies or young children). This might be an unconscious attempt to connect without threat by building rapport with those we encounter.

- Both men and women with lower-pitched voices are perceived as more competent than those who speak with a higher pitch.
- Higher-pitched voices in women are perceived as more attractive, but less competent.
- Use of a wider range of pitch when speaking is perceived as more engaging in both men and women, but also as carrying less authority.

We have to remember that human beings tend to prefer a voice that's not extreme – a 'normal'-sounding voice is genuine, relatable and trustworthy.

But be careful not to move too far away from the real you!

Key considerations

Pause and silence

Silence plays a role in speech – it's what allows our listeners to reflect and soak up what they've heard.

You have the most chance to experiment with pause and its power when you're chairing a conversation, updating a team or organization on significant issues, telling a story or making a presentation. Ten seconds is not too long if you want to emphasize a really important point.

Top tip! When conversing online, maintain some slight movement otherwise people will think your screen has frozen!

A strong accent

Accents in any language can cause other people to form impressions of so many things about us – ethnicity, class, gender, cultural preferences and education, to name a few examples.

If you have an accent, celebrate it for conveying authenticity but try to make sure that it's not so strong that it allows your listeners to switch off from your ideas and messages because they find an accent too difficult to understand or follow. There are readily available resources online to help make any minor adjustments needed to transform a strong accent into an accessible one.

Use simple terms, examples and stories in a well-structured message and you'll give yourself the best opportunity to enable listeners to stay with you.

Paralanguage

This might sound like jargon, but it's simply a 'catch-all' term for anything that isn't words – it includes the music or pitch of the voice, the pace and any habits that form part of the way we speak.

Filler sounds such as 'um' or 'err'

Filler sounds are described by linguists as 'discourse markers', and in conversation they are a demonstration of politeness or consideration, softening the impact of a message or allowing a moment for listeners to reflect. Avoid overuse, however, as the risk is others will stop listening.

I don't ever advocate for complete eradication of filler sounds, as this can make us a bit scripted in our delivery. And on the phone, filler sounds can be an indication that you're still thinking, so they can be useful.

Pace

Pay attention to your pace of speaking. One size doesn't fit all. I know it can feel clunky to rethink an aspect of your communication that has felt instinctive for as long as you can remember, but the more you pay attention to pace, the more natural it will feel to adapt it for your listeners' benefit. Bear in mind though that situation or context may change an approach entirely. You just have to pay attention and decide what's appropriate for your listeners.

Word choices

To make an impact vocally, to underpin the music that enables people to pay attention, you might want to be very intentional with certain key word choices.

In English, consonants carry the conviction of the language (perhaps the best evidence of this is to consider the impact of swearing, which often uses short words that begin and end with consonants and have a single short vowel in the middle), and vowels carry the emotion.

Imagine you're communicating with people in your business and you want to help them understand a significant change – perhaps a rise in the number of customer complaints. Which of the following words might you choose:

- spike (definition: a sharp increase)
- surge (definition: a sudden large increase)?

Say these words out loud and test the impact they have on your delivery. With thoughtful effort and attention to the words you choose, you can significantly improve your impact on your listeners.

Vocal dynamics

We hear our voices conducted through bone and muscle. Bones in the middle ear vibrate as a filter to manage the sound we produce, which would be much louder without this filtering process. Our voice is deepened as a consequence, which is how we hear it.

When we speak, the voice travels through air – producing the very different sound that's heard by others. What we hear recorded is pretty much what everyone else hears, so practice making necessary adjustments to convey the appropriate emotion you need to influence your listeners.

The VAPER model

This model covers the five aspects of voice that offer us an opportunity to adapt and improve so that we're easier to listen to:

V – olume
A – rticulation
P – itch
E – mphasis
R – ate

Volume

- Audibility correlates with credibility. How can you expect your listeners to listen if they can't hear what you say? Bear this in mind with online meetings – you want your listeners to be connected physically and emotionally!
- In face-to-face meetings, make sure you can be easily seen. Avoid looking down at your notes. Maintain eye contact with your listeners and the direction of your voice will follow your gaze, providing more energy and strength. Try not to think too far ahead, as your current sentence or thought will tail away in volume.
- Sit up – you'll need to be able to breathe well to get maximum power in your voice.
- If you need to interrupt, use the other person's name to get their attention before you do so.

Articulation

Ar-tic-u-late! If you want to speak with authority for your listeners, you'll need to put some energy into your word formation. Try doing tongue twisters and pulling shapes with your tongue, lips and face – this tones your speech muscles so you express yourself with clarity, confidence and conviction.

Top tip! Take a work document or slide presentation – something with lots of words and phrases relevant to your business. Read a minute or so of it out loud as fast as you can, but also as accurately as you can. If you make a mistake, go back to the beginning. Make every word precise.

Pitch

Babies and children are hugely expressive with their pitch range, but as we get older, our range reduces.

Top tip! Count from one to ten, alternating each number from the highest point in your pitch range to the lowest – one = high, two = low, three = high, four = low, etc.

Emphasis

Emphasis helps the listener understand your intention and can change the meaning of a sentence. For example try saying the sentence 'I didn't move them' four times by changing the emphasis of each of the four words.

- *I* didn't move them. (It was someone else.)

- I *didn't* move them. (I left them where they were.)
- I didn't *move* them. (I just covered them up.)
- I didn't move *them*. (I moved something else.)

Changing the emphasis on the four different words results in four different sentence meanings.

Rate

If you concentrate on nothing else, get used to adapting your rate to hold your listeners' attention and guide them as you speak.

Choreography

Face-to-face: presenting

Study the space where you plan to present. Use fresh eyes to check the lighting, the seating, the layout of the room. Can it be more comfortable and have fewer distractions?

Then decide how you will choreograph your presentation delivery... what's your position – are you sitting, standing or a bit of both? Make yourself easily seen to help engagement.

Face-to-face: conversations

When you're clear about the type of conversation you want to have and what you want to achieve from the conversation – as well as what you don't want to happen – you can decide which environment will help and how to create it. Whatever you do, make sure it's clear to the other person that this is a listening environment – laptop closed, phones away, table or desk clear of distractions so that there's space for them to sit comfortably and sense that you are fully present.

Where will you sit in relation to the other person? Sitting opposite each other with a desk between you creates a barrier, so check in with yourself to see whether that's going to affect the tone of the conversation and what alternatives might be available or helpful.

Online: ten must-dos for helping your listeners in online communication

1. Invest in equipment – a camera and a microphone – that helps your listeners see you and hear you as clearly as possible.
2. Lighting – don't be lit from behind, or the side.

3. Connect your computer via ethernet cable. Currently, relying on Wi-Fi in online presentations or conversations is not reliable enough.
4. Stand up as often as possible – especially if you're presenting.
5. Check that you are about a newsreader's distance from the camera – make sure you are framed from the waist or chest up; don't let your face fill the screen.
6. Make sure that your eye level is level with the green or blue light next to the camera lens to create a positive impact in conversation. Looking directly down the lens is intimidating for the other person.
7. Invest in a second monitor so you can see everyone on the call.
8. Keep your camera *on*. In a conversation or presentation, this is the best auto-feedback you'll ever get.
9. Set the scene at the beginning of the conversation – tell the other person where you are and what they can expect.
10. Turn off all other potential notifications.

Noticing your listeners' reactions

By minimizing distractions that might get in the way, you'll be free to pay attention to the subtleties and nuances of voice and body language that give you essential information about how the message is landing.

You'll be operating in two environments:

1. **High context:** In the room with your listeners, you'll be able to rely on a rich sensory picture to tell you how things are going, including facial expressions.

    *   Hands: Clenching or gripping, fidgeting or hidden, the hands will be a good starting point for your insight.
    *   Feet: Check for fidgeting, tapping, shuffling, rolling onto the outside of the foot.
    *   Posture: What does a person's overall posture tell you about their energy for the conversation. Are they upright? Rigid? Slumped?

2. **Low context:** Online with your listeners, facial expression, voice and words play a much more powerful role.

- Facial expression: Pursed or tensed lips are a giveaway of tension or disagreement. Check the smile, too – a genuine smile involves the eyes. People who are feeling uncomfortable or awkward will often lick their lips in response to a dry mouth. This is a sign of stress, so tread carefully.

- Eye contact: This is tricky online as we're not able to make direct eye contact at all. One person may be looking at the camera, but they will not be able to pay close attention to the other person on screen. Both people may be looking at the image on screen, which is not making eye contact.

What to do with what you see

Say what you see – and only what you see. This takes courage and practice, but it can unlock a conversation and make it meaningful really quickly – for example: 'I notice your lips are pursed and I'm wondering what might be causing that.' The use of 'I notice...' is helpful. It shows you're paying attention and it will help raise the other person's awareness.

So what? Over to you…

1. Think about an upcoming meeting or presentation. How could you adjust your vocal dynamics – such as pitch, pace and emphasis – to make your communication more engaging and easier for your audience to follow?

2. What steps can you take this week to create a distraction-free and supportive environment for your next important conversation, whether in person or online?

3. What signs, such as body language or vocal tone, could you watch for in your listeners to better understand their reactions and adapt your approach in real time?

Day 10
Concluding with kindness

We all spend most of our working day communicating – listening, talking, writing, reading. Something we take for granted that's so instinctive becomes draining as we unpick our process to improve on technique, develop style and inspire others to make the same changes.

A note of caution as you listen well

I'm a good listener, which means that people reach out to me often. And, because I am committed to listening, I also ask questions. I inquire. I dig a little deeper. I have become less afraid of what I might hear, less afraid of how I might feel when I hear the difficult stuff.

It's therefore vital to look after yourself as a listener. Here's a non-exhaustive list of options that may help you avoid the weight of listener burn-out:

- Observe the shift principle... you'll be listening all day, so try to think in shifts and take breaks.

- If there are days when you're not 'feeling it', be honest where you can and ask to reconvene the conversation. It's rare for everyone to be 'available' to listen fully at the same time.

- Identify a colleague who is a good listener and agree a 'co-listening' shift where you can listen beautifully to each other in the spirit of reciprocity without seeking advice.

- Recognize that excellence ebbs and flows. Be kind to yourself – you won't always get it right.

- Manage your energy! Coffee, sugar and crisps are magnetic beasts... but they don't help our energy as sustained listeners.

- Find a bit of silence for yourself. You're going to be using silence a lot as you pay attention to others, but don't forget to use it to pay attention to yourself.

- You will need to carve out space to breathe... deep, energizing lungfuls of fresh air that give you energy on the way in and take the tension away as you breathe out.

- Save some of your listening skill for those you love... don't burn yourself out listening to people at work and then use your downtime to avoid paying attention at home. If you manage yourself well, your listening skills will enhance all areas of your life.

So what? Over to you...

1. How can you design regular breaks or shifts into the coming week to sustain your energy as a listener?

2. Who could you turn to for support or a 'co-listening' conversation when you need to recharge and reflect this week?

3. How will you recognize when you're reaching your listening limits, and what steps can you take to reset before your next conversation?

Endnotes

[1] D. Goleman, *Emotional Intelligence* (1995).

[2] L. S. Greenberg and W. Malcolm, 'Resolving unfinished business: Relating process to outcome' in *Journal of Counselling and Clinical Psychology*, 70(2), 406–416 (2002).

[3] H. Z. Li, 'Cooperative and intrusive interruptions in inter- and intracultural dyadic discourse' in *Journal of Language and Social Psychology*, 20(3), 259–284.

[4] A. Simmons, *The Story Factor: Inspiration, influence, and persuasion through the art of storytelling* (2001).

[5] C. Booker, *The Seven Basic Plots: Why we tell stories* (2004).

[6] D. Pink, 'The puzzle of motivation', TED talk (2009).

[7] A. Mehrabian, *Silent Messages: Implicit communication of emotions and attitudes* (1972).

Enjoyed this?
Then you'll love…

 *The Listening Shift: Transform your organization by listening to your people and helping your people listen to you* by Janie van Hool

***WINNER BUSINESS SELF-DEVELOPMENT BOOK OF THE YEAR: BUSINESS BOOK AWARDS 2022 ***

As a leader, you work hard at crafting effective messages. You aim to influence, persuade, present. You have a voice, you have a platform… but is anyone listening?

The reality is that the people you're talking to are distracted. They're listening at a rate of 125–250 words per minute, but they're thinking at 1,000–3,000 words per minute. That gap means they're likely to miss 75% of what you say.

And guess what? It's the same when it's your turn to listen. What are you missing? At the very least, if your people don't feel heard or understood by managers and leaders, trust is eroded, frustration increases and engagement is reduced.

You need to listen and be heard...but most of us have never learned how.

The Listening Shift will show you how to be a listening leader. Find out:

- why listening matters
- how to engage people across your organization by listening
- how to have listening conversations – collaborative, connecting and inclusive
- how to help others listen to you.

Janie van Hool is an expert leadership advisor in the art of communication. In the last 20 years, her practical, accessible solutions-focused approach to communicating has allowed hundreds of leaders to engage, inspire and influence their listeners.

Other 6-Minute Smarts titles

 *Building Great Teams* (based on *Workshop Culture* by Alison Coward)

 *Do Change Better* (based on *How to be a Change Superhero* by Lucinda Carney)

 *How to be Happy at Work* (based on *My Job Isn't Working!* by Michael Brown)

 *How to Get to Know Your Customer* (based on *Do Penguins Eat Peaches?* by Katie Tucker)

 *Mastering People Management* (based on *Mission: To Manage* by Marianne Page)

 *No-Nonsense PR* (based on *Hype Yourself* by Lucy Werner)

 *Present Like a Pro* (based on *Executive Presentations* by Jacqui Harper)

 *Reimagine Your Career* (based on *Work/ Life Flywheel* by Ollie Henderson)

 *Sales Made Simple* (based on *More Sales Please* by Sara Nasser Dalrymple)

 *The Speed Storytelling Toolkit* (based on *Exposure* by Felicity Cowie)

 *Write to Think* (based on *Exploratory Writing* by Alison Jones)

Look out for more titles coming soon! Visit www.practicalinspiration.com for all our latest titles.